MW00815133

Pollution Free Environment

Pollution Free Environment

BHUPINDAR SINGH

Copyright © 2021 by Bhupindar Singh.

Library of Congress Control Number: 2021912291

PAPERBACK: 978-1-955955-04-1
EBOOK: 978-1-955955-05-8

All rights reserved. No part of this publication may be reproduced, distributed, or transmitted in any form or by any electronic or mechanical means, without the prior written permission of the publisher, except in the case of brief quotations embodied in critical reviews and certain other noncommercial uses permitted by copyright law.

Ordering Information:

For orders and inquiries, please contact:
1-888-404-1388
www.goldtouchpress.com
book.orders@goldtouchpress.com

Printed in the United States of America

CONTENTS

A Message from the California Public Utilities Commission

Look for a Climate Credit from the State of California on Your April Utility Bill

This month your electricity bill will include a credit identified as the "California Climate Credit." Twice a year, in April and October, your household and millions of others throughout the state will receive this credit on your electricity bills.

The Climate Credit is a payment to Californians from a program designed to fight climate change by limiting the amount of greenhouse gas pollution our largest industries put into the atmosphere.

This program is one of many developed as a result of landmark legislation called the Global Warming Solutions Act of 2006, which puts California at the forefront of efforts to battle climate change. Other programs under this law increase clean, renewable forms of electricity, promote increased energy efficiency in homes and businesses, and require cleaner fuels, and cleaner, more efficient cars and trucks.

Together, these programs will aid in reducing greenhouse gas emissions that trap heat in the atmosphere – helping to clean the air and protect our food, water, and public health, as well as the beauty of our state.

The Climate Credit is designed to help you join with California in its efforts to fight climate change and clean the air. You can use the savings on your electricity bills however you choose, but you can save even more money by investing the bill savings from your Climate Credit in energy-saving home upgrades, including more efficient lights and appliances. You can find more information and receive rebates for these and many other energy efficient choices for your home at www.EnergyUpgradeCA.org/credit.

California's greenhouse gas reduction programs provide a range of powerful solutions to help slow climate change, one of the greatest challenges facing society. By gradually reducing emissions each year and moving to cleaner forms of energy, we are taking an important step to preserve the health and prosperity of our state for generations to come.

The CPUC regulates privately owned electric companies and serves the public interest by protecting consumers and ensuring the provision of safe, reliable utility service and infrastructure at reasonable rates, with a commitment to environmental enhancement and a healthy California economy. For more information about our work contact us at: news@cpuc.ca.gov, 800-253-0500, or visit www.cpuc.ca.gov.

Picture taken : March 17th 2014

Bhupindar Singh: Born Feb. 15. 1932
Email: uoc2@yahoo.com
UNIVERSAL OIL COMPANY (UOC)
Web Site: www. Universaloilcompany.com

Bhupindar Singh, a graduate of the school of Aeronautical Engineering (structures) London, England, came to North America in 1958 and worked for Lockheed Aircraft in Burbank, California. Bhupindar was raised in Tanzania, East Africa, from the age of 3 months to the age of 17 years when he went to England for studies.

In 1997, Buphinder started the Universal Oil Company which specialized in the filtration of lubricant oils used in machinery. UOC's first customer was Tata steel. In 1998, the filtration model and associated unit were installed at Tata's facility in Jamshedpur where dialysis of the entire steel plant systems was performed. The filtration unit removed contaminants from the oil as well as contaminants that had been caked onto the pipes and components immersed in the oil. With the contaminants removed, the oil exerted less frictional forces on the contaminants, thereby prolonging the life of the components as well as the life of the oil itself.

After filtration the oil properties stay similar to new oil, and filtered oil becomes cleaner than new oil. Filtered oil does not have to be discarded for 100 years or more. Thus, land & air do not get contaminated or polluted.

COMPANY PROFILE

The Universal Oil Company's 1000 series filtration system has been designed after conducting a thorough research and development process in the United States. Prior to design, UOC conducted an in-depth survey of various industries including Power & Energy, Iron & Steel and car manufacturing. The objective of this survey was to understand the requirements of the mechanical systems in use by these various industries. UOC's equipment was designed to be as simple and versatile as possible to satisfy the diverse needs of these disparate industries.

UOC takes pride in its position as the provider of the best oil filtration system in Asia. UOC doesn't believe in making lofty promises to its customers that it can't deliver on. The objective of this company is to provide customers with the highest quality system possible. A list of satisfied customers who are willing to testify as to the quality of UOCs system is available.

For countries with emerging economies to gain from this presentation, the mindset of the people must change from;

"WHAT IS IN IT FOR ME?"

TO

"WHAT CAN I DO FOR MY COUNTRY AND

MY PEOPLE?"

High officials and engineers have to have open minds to embrace new concepts, which could be very beneficial.

FOREWORD

Pollution is an ever-growing problem that affects every nation in the world. The information provided here is an attempt to educate decision makers in both the private and public sectors about technology which can help to alleviate some of the pollution caused by the use and disposal of petroleum products. Petroleum products are a critical component of modern infrastructure. They are used as fuel and lubricants in vehicles, industrial machinery and power production equipment as well as countless other applications.

In diesel fuel, gasoline/petrol, diesel oil, motor oil etc., the concentration of contaminants on the scale of 1 to 15 microns is very high. For perspective, the diameter of human hair is approximately 43 microns. There are approximately 140,000,000 (140 million) particles in the 1 to 15 micron range in every liter of new oil. It is unlikely that fuel products have any less contamination than oil products. 40% of these fine particle contaminants do not combust inside of engines and are expelled into the air as pollution by the exhaust system.

Fine filtration of petroleum fuels will remove contaminants to 32,000 particles per 100ml, bringing the concentration down into the region of [less than 140,000,000] per liter. This in effect will increase combustion efficiency, providing better gas mileage, increased power and reduced pollution.

Most of the research in fuels is & has been on control of sulfur emission, but very little on fine particulates. "The size of particles is directly linked to their potential for causing health problems. Small particles less than 10 micrometers in diameter pose the greatest problems, because they can get deep into your lungs, and some may even get into your bloodstream. https://www.epa.gov/pm-pollution/health-and-environmental-effects-particulate-matter-pm

Fine Particulate Matter [PM] pollution is PRIMARY.

"Small particles less than 10 micrometers in diameter pose the greatest problems, because they can get deep into your lungs, and some may even get into your bloodstream."

Fine particulate matter [PM] is a primary form of pollution. Secondary forms of pollution include hydrocarbons, Nitrogen Oxides and Sulfur Dioxide [Sulfur Oxides?]. Diesel exhaust [exhaust from combustion engines?] is a major contributor of PM.

The following article validates my assumptions: https://energyeducation.ca/encyclopedia/Smog

Photochemical smog is a modern phenomena commonly produced by vehicle emissions in contact with sunlight—mostly from burning gasoline and diesel. Photochemical smog forms in warm, densely populated cities with many vehicles.

ACKNOWLEDGEMENTS

I am grateful to my wife Dr. Jagdish Singh [MD], for her support in writing this book. A friend of mine in London, Mr. Manmohan Singh, encouraged me a great deal in my efforts on this book, as did Mr. Deepak Gandhi.

I am very thankful to my brother, Mr. Kulbir Singh and Tejai Singh and Chris Pinkham, who read and helped me edit this book. Also, I acknowledge the contributions of various researchers and engineers from whose works and researches I have taken their input to provide authenticity to the written information in this book.

CAUSES OF POLLUTION

Coal

Coal fires, used to heat individual buildings or in a power-producing plant, can emit significant clouds of smoke that contributes to smog. Air pollution from this source has been report in England since the Middle Ages. London, in particular, was notorious through the mid-20th century for its coal-caused smogs, which were nicknamed 'pea-soupers.' Air pollution of this type is still a problem in areas that generate significant smoke from burning coal, as witnessed by the 2013 autumnal smog in Harbin, China, which closed roads, schools, and the airport.

Transportation emissions

Traffic emissions – such as from trucks, buses, and automobiles – also contribute. Airborne by-products from vehicle exhaust systems cause air pollution and are a major ingredient in the creation of smog in some large cities.

Photochemical smog

Photochemical smog was first described in the 1950s. It is the chemical reaction of sunlight, nitrogen oxides and volatile organic compounds in the atmosphere, which leaves airborne particles and ground-level ozone. This noxious mixture of air pollutants can include the following:

<u>Aldehydes</u>
Nitrogen oxides, such as nitrogen dioxide
Peroxyacyl nitrates
Tropospheric ozone
<u>Volatile organic compounds</u>

Characteristic coloration of smog in California is the beige cloud bank behind the Golden Gate Bridge. The brown coloration is due to the NOx in the photochemical smog.

Natural causes

An erupting volcano can also emit high levels of sulphur dioxide along with a large quantity of particulate matter; two key components to the creation of smog. However, the smog created as a result of a volcanic eruption is often known as vog to distinguish it as a natural occurrence.

HEALTH EFFECTS

Highland Park Optimist Club wearing smog-gas masks at banquet, Los Angeles, circa 1954. The air quality in Los Angeles at this time was considered so poor, people had to wear gas masks to breath. This should not be the direction for our future generations.

INTRODUCTION

By the late 1960's smog became a major issue in California. This was especially true in Los Angeles and surrounding cities. It was not uncommon for smog to be so thick, that one could not see the massive San Gabriel mountains located a mere three miles from down town Los Angeles. The air reeked with pollution and there were many reports the polluted air irritated people's eyes and respiratory systems.

In response to the smog crisis California started implementing clean air enforcement. All vehicles in or entering California had to have filtered diesel or unleaded fuel. This was strictly monitored and enforced. By the late 1980's clean air policies in California had resulted in substantial improvements to air quality. The mountains could once again be seen from Los Angeles and the air was no longer irritating. Even though the air quality is much better than in the days which prompted pollution control measures, there are still days when a blanket of smog envelopes Los Angeles.

A major reason for this continued pollution is that 40% of these 1 to 15 micron fine particle contaminants do not burn during combustion and are exhausted into the air. These particles cause various ailments such as asthma, eye and respiratory irritation and cancer among others. The effects of fine particle pollution are particularly severe in developing nations such as China, India and Thailand where less air quality regulations are in effect. These ailments would decrease in prevalence if pollution is reduced. In order to control pollution further, fuel has to be filtered and 1 to 15 micron particle contaminants have to be decreased by further filtration in a 1 micron filter.

In economically growing countries such as China, India, Thailand, etc., pollution spewed out by petroleum products is causing ailments such as Asthma, Eye Irritation, Sore Throat, Cancer, and other dangerous diseases.

All these ailments could be lessened considerably with a cleaner environment.

AGRICULTURE

Various types of industrial oils are dumped on the ground in many growing economies, causing considerable damage to water and air resulting in less fertile ground. This damages the quality of produce, which, in turn, causes more health related problems.

INDUSTRIAL ASSET MANAGEMENT THROUGH OUT THE WORLD ----- PRODUCES CLEAN ENVIORNMENT

Would you like to have a relatively maintenance free production in Plants where oil is used extensively in equipment & for the production of different products?

Millions of dollars are spent in procuring different equipment in various industries.

It is a pity that engineers are not aware of how to prolong the life of machinery and oil used in it. Power Plant turbines, hydraulic systems, car engines, equipment having gear oil are examples. **IF CONTROL OF 1 to 15 MICRON Contaminants are controlled, then all the above systems will have less friction allowing for a longer lifespan of the systems.**

TRIBOLOGY IS A SCIENCE OF FRICTION CONTROL to ENHANCE EQUIPMENT LIFE.

Tribology and Its Essential
Progress in the Successful Operation of Machines

The subject of this writing will explain a term that is relatively new based on an element in Greek that is used in modern engineering and physics:

Tribology. This Greek **tribo**- element means "friction, rub, and grind "or" to wear away".

Lubrication is central to machine performance, but it's only one part of the story. More and more, the bigger picture of machine health has been ignored.

- Tribology combines issues of **lubrication**, **friction**, and **wear** into a complex framework for designing, maintaining, and trouble-shooting the whole machine world.

- Tribology is already providing data that could be used to produce transmission fluids that give automobile drivers better fuel economy and a smoother ride.

- The most visionary tribology advocates and practitioners tend to view their field as the cure for much of what ails industry and even entire economies.

- *Oxford English Dictionary* defines tribology as, "The branch of science and technology concerned with interacting surfaces in relative motion and with associated matters. (like friction, wear, lubrication, and the design of bearings).

Nomenclature:

NAS—National Aerospace Standard.

Close Tolerance: Extremely close gaps between two moving parts.

Lapping compound: Like Emory Paper Rubbing.

Journal Bearing: Like a rod having bearings at both ends.

SILT

Particles of 1-2 microns are not considered in **NAS level** determination. However, they are just as dangerous as 5-15 micron particles.

UOC **filtration removes large numbers of 1-2 micron particles**, known as **silt**, which cause **considerable wear** to close tolerance parts and cause **internal leakages**, thereby **lowering system efficiency**.

The oil in the system travels at **very high pressure and speed and the silt causes considerable wear to the valves and seals**.

These silt particles act like bullets, causing **Lapping Compound like action.**

By controlling silt, **friction** in machinery is considerably reduced, thus giving longer life and trouble free production.

- 85% of problems in equipment is due to highly contaminated oil with silt.

- **Increased equipment life means millions of dollars saved.**

Silt in New oil [**1-2 micron** particles] is approximately **13,000,000/100 ml.**

In used oil, silt could be as much as **3 to 7 times more**.

Therefore, used oil, even brought to NAS "4", would have a wear rate at least **10 times more than New oil [just like dirty oil]**, unless 1 -2 micron particles are **brought down to the level of New oil**.

Transmissions are just one place where tribology makes a difference in the automotive industry.

Other items on the agenda include controlling brake noise and wear, reducing internal friction in engines, increasing the productivity, part quality, and energy efficiency of production machinery.

What Is Silt Lock?

Silt lock is when micron-sized particles (silt) become lodged between the hydraulic valve spool and the bore. Silt particles migrate into the clearances between the spool and bore, increasing friction when the valve is actuated when more and more of these silt particles become lodged in the clearances. It eventually results in silt lock.

Silt lock stops production, increases valve maintenance costs and slows production due to sluggish response. Setting up a lubrication program to control contamination will prevent this from happening.

The presence of varnish on valve spools and bores tightens the interference fit (annular clearance), reducing the particle size affecting contaminant lock.

The varnish also has adherent properties that stick the particles to the silt lands.

The longer a valve holds pressure without actuation, the longer the available time for the valve to silt up (and sludge up).

Most stiction-related valve failures occur just after a long dwell time. Large amounts of silt-sized particles in the 1- to 5 –micron range have a tendency to grow dramatically in population as oils age.

These clearance-sized particles increase the propensity of contaminant lock.

Water has a tendency to preferentially coat particles. Two such particles in contact will cling together (like wet sand), aggravating the silt-lock risk considerably.

"FOR ENGINEERS"

Cleanliness Requirements for Journal Bearing Lubrication

Refrences:

Kelly Collins, Pall Corporation John Duchowski, Pall Corporation

THE STUDY OF JOURNAL BEARING

The minimum film thickness is found at the closest point of contact between the journal and the sleeve.

Theoretical analysis reveals that for these journal- bearing sizes under normal operating conditions, a 1 - 20 microns thick hydrodynamic film forms to separate the journal from the pads, since film thickness is dependent on fluid viscosity.

As the fluid temperature rises, the film thickness may be reduced by as much as 20% for some lubricants.

Theoretical analysis shows the minimum film thickness is between 1-20 microns; however, empirical results reveal that even though dimensional clearances within a journal bearing may differ, and the load and rotational speed may vary, the **actual film thickness is in the order of approximately 10 microns**.

Abrasive wear occurs when **clearance-sized particles come between two surfaces** that are **under load**, such as in the journal and the bearing.

These tests were conducted over a 20-hour period with interruptions for wear measurements, at five hour intervals.

It can be seen that **more than a ten-fold increase in bearing wear** results from contaminated oil.

The filtration requirement is most critical at the commissioning of turbines, compressors or other equipment and when the equipment **is rotating at low rpm**. It is at these times that the **hydrodynamic film is the thinnest.**

Unfortunately, some equipment designers tend to consider the overall capital costs rather than the technical requirements of the system when choosing filtration systems. Field experience has proven that this approach can result in much higher operating costs when the costs for repairs, maintenance, parts replacement and lost production are considered.

Given that the film thickness that exists under normal operating conditions is **approximately 10 microns**, and since **the film thickness is further reduced during startup** and at low viscosity condition or with lower viscosity fluids, it is recommended that the filter employed exhibit a high removal efficiency of particles **down to 5 microns or finer.**

DESCRIPTION OF UOC FILTERS

UOC Filters are specially designed to reduce the friction in the oil by filtering out all the contaminants from the oil. These filters are called Depth Type Filters. Beta ratio of these filters is 99.99. Most of the oil systems found in the industries are at NAS 12+ level which in itself has more than 1 million particles of 5 to 15 microns. Even new oil available in the market is at NAS 10-12 level. UOC filters not only filter out these and larger particles but they also filter out particles of 1 and 2 micron sizes which are not considered for NAS value calculations. Given below is the contamination chart:

New Oil

ISO Code	9/6	10/7	12/9	13/10	14/11	16/13	12/18
National Aerospace Standards (NAS)	0	1	3	4	5	7	12
Size Range (Micron)	Values based per 100 ml						
5-15	250	500	2000	4000	8000	32000	1024000
15-25	22	88	356	712	1425	5700	182400
25-50	4	16	63	126	253	1012	33400
50-100	1	3	11	22	45	180	5760
Over 100	0	1	2	4	8	32	1024

SILT

System efficiency:

The oil in the system travels at very high pressure and speed, the silt causes Particles of 1-2 microns that are not considered in NAS level determination. However, they are just as dangerous as 5-15 micron particles. UOC filtration removes large numbers of 1-2 micron particles, known as silt, which cause considerable wear to close tolerance parts and cause internal leakages, thereby increasing wear to the valve seals. These silt particles act like bullets, causing Lapping Compound like action, similar to a Emory board or sand paper.

HOW CONTAMINATED OIL DESTROYS EQUIPMENT

Solids suspended in oil are like grinding paste.

They scour and gouge surfaces; block oil passages and makes the oil more viscous. The longer the oil is left dirty the faster the rate of failure.

Many **original equipment manufacturers** have accepted the indisputable evidence from numerous field and laboratory trials that **oil cleanliness has a major effect on wear within their equipment.**

Some of them are now specifying how clean the oil used in their equipment should be if warranty claims are to be honoured.

For example Caterpillar specifies new oil to have a particle count of ISO 16/13 or NAS 7.

If new oil is above this level of contamination they will not warranty their equipment.

When new oil from a leading international oil manufacturer was tested before putting it into new Caterpillar equipment , the solid particle contamination was found to be 17/14. This was new oil from a never previously opened container.

In this case the new oil had to be further filtered to bring it below the required specification.

If you want extremely low wear rates and long equipment life the evidence indicates that **oil** needs to **be filtered down** to sub 5 micron size and preferably **down to one micron size.**

For **expensive hydraulic and oil lubricated equipment filtration cost is easily and quickly recuperated by the large gain in equipment working life and reliability.**

HOW CONTAMINATION DESTROYS ENGINES

New oil is NAS 12 Fig. (A) Directly below, the black patch is figure is oil tested after running engine on test stand for 45 minutes. This oil has become unsafe. It should be filtered with 1 micron Depth Filter or replaced with new oil. Figure (D) is cleaner than new oil in Figure (A), after filtration of Figure (C) oil, On the extreme upper right figure (E), 1 micron depth filter attached to engine while running on test stand, resulting in very clean oil.

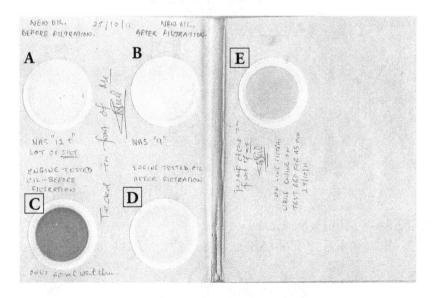

Universal Oil Company

UNIVERSAL OIL COMPANY

NAS 12+
LUBE A
SAMPLE POINT- 615 MM ABOVE TANK BOTTOM 320 VISCOSITY
40 ML PASSED THROUGH MEMBRANE
26-10-2010

NAS 12+
LUBE B
TANK CAPACITY-2500 LTRS
320 VISCOSITY
40ML PASSED THROUGH MEMBRANE 26-10-2010

Lube A — Mill Drive Gear Boxes
Lube B — R E S & Cold Shear

Lube "A" oil sample was taken from Pump Suction Chamber [615 up from bottom of tank]. This oil is After Filtration from an external filtration unit.

Millipore test was conducted in front of Mr. V Kudva. Only 40 ml of fluid passed through the membrane. The rest of the fluid [60 mm] was discarded.

Lube "B" oil sample was tested. Again only 40 ml of fluid passed through the membrane. Sample was taken from the sampling point, near the drain point.. To this system no external filtration is attached.

Test Results :
Tremendous amount of Silt
Shiny metal particles
Oil is NAS 12+

Comments — Oil is not fit for use, and has already started damaging the internals of both the systems.

Solution — Oil should be drained from both the systems and stored in drums. After couple of weeks the contamination will settle at the bottom of drums, and the oil then syphoned off 10" from drum bottoms, and oil put into fresh drums. This oil can then be used as fresh oil for topping up, etc.

With silt control – no wear at all (no
scoring at all – shaft is smooth)
Figure 2. **Silt** Control
Oil is NAS 4 – 5
This picture was magnified

without silt control – wear on spool
(scoring on the spool)
Figure 1. **No Silt** Control
Oil is NAS 4 – 5

Pictures Provided By Tata Steel After 5 Years Of once A Month Filtration.

Universal Oil Company has been doing
Turbine and Hydraulic oil filtration for last 14 years.

Universal Oil Company case study on silt control. [2006]

Ref: SMMM/285/13
Date: 4/10/13

To whom it may Concern

TATA STEEL FINDINGS OF BENEFITS OF FILTRATION, BY USING **UNIVERSAL OIL COMPANY** [UOC]
FILTRATION UNIT, **THAT ALSO CONTROLS SILT** [1—5 micron contamination].

Using Universal Oil Company [UOC] Filtration Unit, we have found that system performance of Hydraulic
Power Packs and Controls, and of Captive Power Plants, Turbine and Turbine Controls, have **increased**.

We also found:

a] increased life of components immersed in oil.
b] Increased life of built-in filters in our systems.
c] increased life of oil, for an extended period due to control of silt. With proper filtration, all oil
properties remain the same.
d] Wear and tear of components immersed in oil, slowed down
e] No more leakages from joints, seals etc., and provided damaged parts are replaced.
f] Less maintenance manpower utilized.
g] Maximum efficiency for production is ensured.

NOTE: We found **no adverse effects** in all our systems due to control of silt and maintaining NAS level
below 5

The above benefits give **more profits** to the company.

Sunil Kumar Mishra
(Chief, Steel Making Mechanical Maintenance)

TATA STEEL LIMITED
Jamshedpur 831 001 India
Registered Office Bombay House 24 Homi Mody Street Mumbai 400 001

21

Bhupindar Singh

PROUD TO BE INDIAN
PRIVILEGED TO BE GLOBAL

To whomsoever it may concern:

Universal oil Company has performed filtration of our Press power pack and has brought the system oil to NAS 7 from NAS 14, in an environment that is extremely dirty, where fine dust from graphite is present in the air. Also simultaneously controlled silt [1 to 2 micron contamination particles], which is very harmful to all the components immersed in oil.

We have now purchased the filtration unit from UOC and attached it permanently to the power pack. Now the system oil is maintained to NAS 6.

We are satisfied with the performance of UOC filtration unit.

Sanjay Dubey

HEG LIMITED

Plant & Regd. Office :
Mandideep (Near Bhopal)
Distt. Raisen - 462046. (M.P.), India
Tel. : +91-7480-233524 to 233527
Fax : +91-7480-233522
E-mail : heg.mdp@lnjbhilwara.com

Corporate Office :
Bhilwara Towers, A-12, Sector-1
Noida - 201 301 (NCR-Delhi), India
Tel. : +91-120-4390300 (EPABX)
Fax : +91-120-4277841
Website : www.hegltd.com

DEPTH TYPE FILTRATION UNIT HAVING 1 MICRON PAPER FILTER USED FOR CONTROLLING CONTAMINANTS OF 1 MICRON & UP.

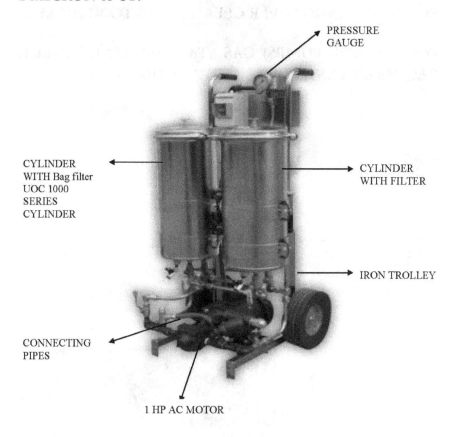

PRESSURE GAUGE

CYLINDER
WITH Bag filter
UOC 1000
SERIES
CYLINDER

CYLINDER
WITH FILTER

IRON TROLLEY

CONNECTING
PIPES

1 HP AC MOTOR

REQUIREMENT FOR GAS PUMPS (PETROL PUMPS), TO CONVERT

FOR DISPENCING SUPER CLEAN FUELS TO VEHICLES.

FOR (PETROL PUMPS) GAS STATIONS TO CONVERT, REQUIRE 2 TANKS OF 1.5 AND 2.0 CUBIC METERS.

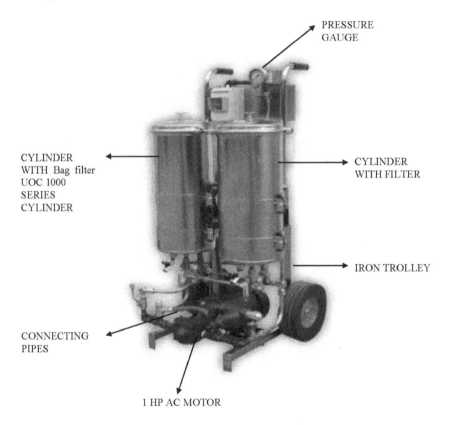

PRESSURE GAUGE

CYLINDER WITH Bag filter UOC 1000 SERIES CYLINDER

CYLINDER WITH FILTER

IRON TROLLEY

CONNECTING PIPES

1 HP AC MOTOR

UNIVERSAL OIL COMPANY (UOC) IS AVAILABLE FOR CONSULTATION

The two tanks should be connected to each other, and 2.0 cubic tank (A) should be connected to the fuel tank underground.

The fuel is pumped from the underground tank into tank A, where the fuel will be filtered and pumped into smaller tank (B).

Tank B will be connected to petrol (gas or fuel) pump, from where the fuel will be pumped into vehicles.

One micron depth filter should be used for filtration.

FUEL ADDITIVE

Organically Manufactured Diesel/Petrol (Gas) Fuel Additive patented by Parshum Ram Niranjan Shastri

THE DIESEL FUEL HAS ABOUT 25%TO 40% CONTAMINANTS INCLUDING SULFUR THAT DO NOT BURN WHEN THE COMBUSTION TAKES PLACE.

When diesel fuel additive is added to the diesel fuel, the additive acts as a catalyst whereby all the contaminants including sulfur evaporate due to oxidation process. During combustion 99% of the fuel burns, thereby giving better mileage and clean air is coming out of the engine.

The Cetane of the fuel increases also.

The ingredients in Diesel Fuel Additive are following Organic Minerals:

Diethyl Malonate
Diethylene Triamine Pentaacetic Acid
Dimethylformamide
Sodium Carbonate
Sodium Hydroxide

Other benefits are, that diesel does not get bacteria growth, and the vehicle injector system stays absolutely clean and lubricated.

Newport Lexus	(949) 477-7000
3901 MacArthur Blvd.	(949) 477-7010 Fax
Newport Beach, CA 92660	www.newportlexus.com

July 25, 2018

Mr. Singh,

I'm writing to provide you with the results I experienced during my road trip after using the fuel injection cleaner. I want to start by saying that I've never used any type of fuel injection cleaner in my car which is a 2015 Toyota Prius and I typically use 89 grade fuels from Chevron.

At the time the road trip began my odometer read 47,107 miles. For this trip I was driving from California to Idaho which is approximately 868 miles one way. The driving conditions were normal with the exception of a head wind for approximately 125 miles.

On average while in town I have a 16 mile commute which consists of the 405 and 5 freeways. During this commute I average 38.2 miles per gallon. While using the suggested amount of fuel injection cleaner per fill up and a total of three refuels during my trip, I averaged 42/43 miles per gallon which was an increase of 4/5 miles per gallon.

I'm currently at 51,598 miles and since that trip have not used any fuel injection cleaner. I'm currently averaging 38.6 miles to the gallon.

Sincerely,

Jason Johnson
Service Director
Newport Lexus
3901 Mac Arthur Blvd.
Newport Beach, Ca. 92660
jasonjohnson@newportlexus.com
949-477-7080 direct

The above odometer reading shows at 70 miles per hour shows 30.7 miles per gallon. This mileage is obtained in 100 miles drive in my Genesis GS80, after I put fuel additive into the fuel tank. I normally got about 24 miles per gallon.

COAL ENHANCER

by P N SHASTRI

The optimum mesh size of the coal to be sprayed somewhere between 0 and 10 inches across.

O Process high, medium or low level radioactive coal combustion by-product (CCP) waste from coal mining and coal fired power plants.

O Increase energy output by 8-12%.

O **WITH 3 FILTERS IN THE STACK, THE FOLLOWING IMPROVEMENTS CAN BE OBTAINED**

O Decrease Sulfur contents to the Indian Govt. requirement

O Reduce emission such as NO_x, SO_x, CO, CO_2 and other particulates matters (PM).

O Treated coal is burnt more efficiently increasing energy output 8 -12%.

O No waste products, not hot air, water or steam.

O 95% reduction of air emissions and remainder of resulting gases are neutral.

O No waste products that requires disposal.

O Fly ash captured in Fly Ash Filter reduces by 75% to 100% Fly ash hazardous materials, and emissions become harmless.

O Bottom ash becomes not-hazardous after treatment and post combustion filter. It can be used in cement industry or can be used for fertilizer.

O Process allows blended fly ash (form sub-bituminous and bituminous coals) to meet ASTM requirements for use in cement applications.

O Dr. P.N. Shastri coal enhancer is a biotech enzyme product for reducing SOX, NOX, CO2 emissions and preventing corrosion.

O Coal enhancer is specially engineered for use on coal. The enzyme acts as a catalyst, allowing the coal to obtain various beneficial qualities such as improved combustion efficiency, reduced greenhouse gas emission and reduced byproducts.

• Reduces future accumulation of coking.	• Reduces duration of scheduled maintenance.
• Micro dispersion of heavy metal impurities to form complex soft ionic salts	• Reduced duration of scheduled maintenance.

• Reduces high/low temperature corrosion	• Reduced shutdown translates to increased uptime, increased production of time and ultimately increased profits.
• Prevents calories loss and spontaneous combustion of coal during storage for up to 6 months	• Enables prolonged storage of coal stockpiles. • Allows for larger order of coal, enabling price savings.

O Biocracking

  O The Biocracking process breaks the coal hydrocarbons bonds and decomposes hydrocarbon and Sulphur compounds. They rapidly decompose to fine particle molecules which burn more effectively and improve efficiency.

  O Coal Enhancer contains biological active ingredients that modify the coal so that under high temperature, it will actively and rapidly react, forming amorphous crystal micro-explosions within that break down the coal on a molecular level. This helps to achieve complete and more efficient combustion.

  O The catalytic processes of the enzymes causes coal particles to be surrounded with oxygen molecules. It reduces the ignition point and provides extra free oxygen to improve combustion. It reduces the demand for air intake (oxygen), maintains energy supply and lowers stack heat loss.

○ Reduction of sulfur oxide (SOx) by desulfurization.

   ○ During coal combustion in the furnace, Coal Enhancer catalyzes the formation of sodium sulfate and solid calcium sulfate by oxidation of sulfur dioxide with sodium and calcium ions, which reduces the emission of sulfur oxides.

○ Principle s of desulfurization

   ○ The biological enzymes in Coal Enhancer can crack the bonds between carbon to carbon (c-c) and Carbon to sulfur (c-s) and produce oxygen, carbon, hydrogen compounds and sulfate by products etc.

   ○ The desulfurization process is achieved by the catalytic process between bacteria.

   ○ The biological enzyme catalysts do not form any toxic byproducts or side reactions.

○ Reduction of nitrogen oxides (NOX)

   ○ Nitrogen is found in abundance and makes up 78% of the atmosphere.

   ○ Nitrogen is a major component of NOX.

   ○ The NOX is formed under combustion conditions at temperatures above 700°C, and a small portion of the nitrogen oxide is from nitrogen compounds in the oily molecules of the coal itself.

- The use of the Coal Enhancer stabilizes the oxidized nitrogen compounds.

- In addition, due to the improved combustion efficiency of the coal in Low Excess Air Combustion, the air intake required for combustion is lowered; hence less nitrogen is introduced during combustion, resulting in reduced NOX being produced.

- Low temperature corrosion is due to conversion of sulfur dioxide to sulfur trioxide, causing sulfuric acid to form while reacting with steam in furnace.

  - Coal Enhancer micro disperse sulfur, nitrogen and phosphorus compound.

  - Sulfur is converted to Sulfate (nitrate ions and compounds) which reduce the amount of SO2 and SO3.

- The presence of extra oxygen formed by Coal Enhancer catalytic process actively penetrated into the coke accumulated in combustion chamber walls and surfaces, enabling the residual combustible carbon in the coke to be burned.

- The use of Coal Enhancer creates a higher pH (pH=8.5) environment in the combustion chamber, causing the accumulated coke to separate and lose its adhesive strength.

- Under high temperature (1,100°C), the coke and carbon deposits are loosened from the surfaces, leaving behind a dry solid film that protects the furnace walls from corrosion.

○ Carbon deposits reduce the lifespan and output potential of equipment, affecting not only heat transfer, but also seals, air flow, burner nozzle and emissions.

○ Through the process of micro dispersion, Coal Enhancer improves coal combustion and feed condition, and reduction of carbon deposits in the furnace.

○ It forms a protective layer that protects burner nozzles and metal surfaces.

○ The advanced bio cleaning formula cleans up the nozzle, combustion chamber and exhaust system.

Dr. Parshu Ram Niranjan Shastri
Bhupindar Singh
1 818 207 1534

GREEN COAL TECHNOLOGY

Coal Enhancer
S168 Biotech Enzyme
product for reducing SOX,
NOX and CO2 emissions

Green Coal Treatment Flow

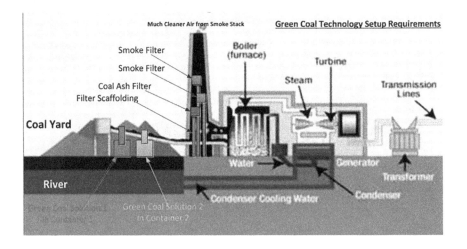

O After treatment of Coal with solutions 1 and 2 the reaction process will take 5 - 7 minutes to complete before burning in the furnace.

Green Coal Setup Requirements

- Green Coal Setup Requirements:

    - 1. Need a container with jet spray mechanism for Green Coal Solution 1

    - 2. Need a container with jet spray mechanism for Green Coal Solution 2

    - 3. Need two (2) Smoke Filters install within the first half of the total height of the smoke stack.

    - 4. Need One (1) Coal S Filter install in the lower half of the smoke stack.

    - 5. Need to install Scaffolding for the 3 filters inside the Smoke Stack.

    - 6. The optimum mesh size of the coal to be sprayed somewhere between 0 and 10 inches across.

Green Coal Treatment Protocol

- Crush coal is sprayed with CA-C water-based solution and treated as coal passes along conveyor.

- CA-C treatment solution requires 1 liter of diluted solution per ton of coal.

- Process does not affect speed of normal coal combustion process. We can adjust or load according to coal throughput.

- Process is not sensitive to changes in fuel, plant operations, variations in load or unit outages; Process is highly flexible and operated per load demand.

- 400- 500 sq-ft (40 sq-m) area required for processing equipment. Equipment is integrated into the pre-boiler combustion process.

- Fly Ash Filter and Bottom Ash Filter have 2 year replacement insert layer of proprietary compounds.

COAL INDUSTRY OUTLOOK

Consumption of Coal Around The World

Consumption of Coal and lignite in 2014

Year: 2014	Unit: Million tons
China	3,473
India	924
United States	835
Germany	236
Russia	211
South Africa	197
Japan	184
South Korea	134
Poland	130
Australia	122

Coal Industry Challenges

- Coal consumption is considered as major source of global warming

- New and tougher anti-coal regulations are being enacted

- Discontinuation of funding for coal projects are being issued.

- Closure of power plants and coal mines starting to happen

- Potentially putting billion of people without electricity

- There is no technology capable of meeting the new regulations

- Carbon Capture and Sequestration is not an answer

WHAT IS THE SOLUTION TO THE CHALLENGES?

Green Coal Treatment

Green Coal Treatment will:

O Process high, medium or low level radioactive coal combustion by-product (CCP) waste from coal mining and coal fired power plants.

O Increase energy output by 8-12%.

O Decrease Sulfur contents to almost zero.

O Completely reduce emission such as NOx, SOx, CO, CO2 and other particulates (PM).

Pounds of CO2 emitted per million British Thermal Units (BTU) of energy for various Fuels:

Fuel Type:	Pounds of CO2 emitted
Coal (anthracite)	228.6
Coal (bituminous)	205.7
Coal (lignite)	215.4
Coal (subbituminous)	214.3
Diesel fuel and heating Oil	161.3
Gasoline	157.2
Propane	139.0
Natural Gas	117.0
Green Coal w/ coal enhancer	Almost 0.0

Green Coal Treatment Benefits

○ Treated coal is burnt more efficiently increasing energy output 8 -12%.

○ No waste products, not hot air, water or steam.

○ 95% reduction of air emissions and remainder of resulting gases are neutral.

○ No waste products that requires disposal.

○ Fly ash captured in Fly Ash Filter reduces 100%Fly ash hazardous materials and emissions become harmless.

○ Bottom ash becomes not-hazardous after treatment and post combustion filter. It can be used in cement industry or can be used for fertilizer.

○ Process allows blended fly ash (form sub-bituminous and bituminous coals) to meet ASTM requirements for use in cement applications.

Green Coal Treatment Budget

O End user funds full-scale installation, we can provide demonstration model.

O Cost of sprayer and filters is dependent upon size of existing combustion system.

O CA-C mineral compound will be priced by the ton and will be packaged as concentrated in burlap (jute) bags in barrels and shipped by container, to dilute in water.

O CA-C jelly cost may vary depending on quality of coal used and price fluctuations in raw materials.

O The increase in energy output will cover the ongoing cost of CA-C supply and manufacture of sprayer and filters.

O This is a Net-Revenue to operate process.

DR. P.N. SHASTRI COAL ENHANCER S168

The very first biotech enzyme for reducing SOX, NOX, CO2 emissions and preventing corrosion.

Coal Enhancer S168

O Dr. P.N. Shastri coal enhancer is a biotech enzyme product for reducing SOX, NOX, CO2 emissions and preventing corrosion.

O Coal enhancer is specially engineered for use on coal. The enzyme acts as a catalyst, allowing the coal to obtain various beneficial qualities such as improved combustion efficiency, reduced greenhouse gas emission and reduced byproducts.

Features	Benefits
• Improve coal combustion efficiency	• Coal consumption saving between 3 to 15%. This is dependent on the type of coal and furnace used.
• Reduces the amount of air intake required ,reduces oxygen content of exhaust by about 25%	• With reduced consumption, companies will also benefit from reduced carbon emissions resulting in significant savings from any carbon tax in Australia.
• Reduces carbon content in slag by 10% to 20%	
• Reduces stack gas heat loss and increases furnace temperatures by 50°C to 200°C	
• Increase coal's fusion point, prevents furnace wall coking and improves heat transfer	

• Reduces sulfur compounds (SOX) by 30% to 60%	• Reduce greenhouse gas emissions
• Reduces nitrogen compounds (NOX)	• Greener and more environmentally friendly operations.
• Ringelmann scale lower by 3 levels	
• Reduces sludge salt in the slag by 20% to 50%	
Removes coking and carbon deposits in combustion chamber walls, heat exchange surfaces and other mechanical parts	Reduce frequency of downtime from shutdown for maintenance.
• Reduces future accumulation of coking.	• Reduces duration of scheduled maintenance.
• Micro dispersion of heavy meatal impurities to form complex soft ionic salts	• Reduced duration of scheduled maintenance.
• Reduces high/low temperature corrosion	• Reduced shutdown translates to increased uptime, increased production of time and ultimately increased profits.
• Prevents calories loss and spontaneous combustion of coal during storage for up to 6 months.	• Enables prolonged storage of coal stockpiles. Allows for larger order of coal, enabling price savings.

Bhupindar Singh

How does Coal Enhancer improve coal combustion efficiency?

O Biocracking

O The Biocracking process breaks the coal hydrocarbons bonds and decomposes hydrocarbon and Sulphur compounds. They rapidly decompose to fine particle molecules which burn more effectively and improve efficiency.

O Coal Enhancer contains biological active ingredients that modify the coal so that under high temperature, it will actively and rapidly react, forming amorphous crystal micro-explosions within that break down the coal on a molecular level. This helps to achieve complete and more efficient combustion.

O The catalytic processes of the enzymes causes coal particles to be surrounded with oxygen molecules. It reduces the ignition point and provides extra free oxygen to improve combustion. It reduces the demand for air intake (oxygen), maintains energy supply and lowers stack heat loss.

Coal Enhance Combustion Efficiency

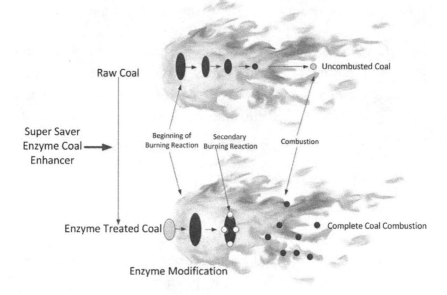

How does Coal Enhancer reduce Sulfur Oxides?

O Reduction of sulfur oxide (SOx)by desulfurization.

   O During coal combustion in the furnace, Coal Enhancer catalyzes the formation of sodium sulfate and solid calcium sulfate by oxidation of sulfur dioxide with sodium and calcium ions, which reduces the emission of sulfur oxides.

O Principle s of desulfurization

   O The biological enzymes in Coal Enhancer can crack the bonds between carbon to carbon (c-c)and Carbon to sulfur (c-s)and produce oxygen, carbon, hydrogen compounds and sulfate by products etc.

   O The desulfurization process is achieved by the catalytic process between bacteria.

   O The biological enzyme catalysts do not form any toxic byproducts or side reactions.

How Does Coal Enhancer Reduce Nitrogen Oxides?

O Reduction of nitrogen oxides (NOX)

　　O Nitrogen is found in abundance and makes up 78% of the atmosphere.

　　O Nitrogen is a major component of NOX.

　　O The NOX is formed under combustion conditions at temperatures above 700°C, and a small portion of the nitrogen oxide is from nitrogen compounds in the oily molecules of the coal itself.

　　O The use of the Coal Enhancer stabilizes the oxidized nitrogen compounds.

　　O In addition, due to the improved combustion efficiency of the coal in Low Excess Air Combustion, the air intake required for combustion is lowered; hence less nitrogen is introduced during combustion, resulting in reduced NOX being produced.

Sulfide Oxidation Process

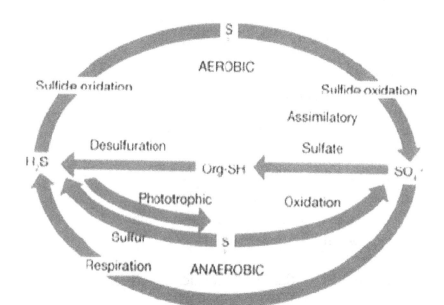

How does Coal Enhancer reduce high/low temperature corrosion?

O Low temperature corrosion is due to conversion of sulfur dioxide to sulfur trioxide, causing sulfuric acid to form while reacting with steam in furnace.

    O Coal Enhancer micro disperse sulfur , nitrogen and phosphorus compound.

    O Sulfur is converted to Sulfate (nitrate ions and compounds) which reduce the amount of SO_2 and SO_3.

O High temperature corrosion is caused by the presence of V_2O_5 under high temperature conditions.

    O Salts like sodium chloride form Na_2SO_4 and are suspended in combustion chamber and exhausts. Sulfate forms Mg_2SO_4, $7H_2O$ and other similar compounds, forms with barium (Ba) and reacts further with V_2O_5 to form $Mg_3V_2O_8$ (mp. 1191°C).

    O The enzymes in Coal Enhancer prevents those detrimental substances to agglomerate and molten under high temperature corrosion by keeping them in solid inert ash, making them bulk and easy to clean up form the furnace chamber.

How does Coal Enhancer Reduce calorie loss and prevent spontaneous combustion in stockpiles?

O Such phenomena are created by anaerobic methanobacteriaceae bacteria and sulfate-reducing bacteria within the coal that normally lay dormant in its natural state.

   O Once the coal is unearthed, these bacteria begin feeding off the coal (creating calorie loss) and breeding at and exponential rate, creating increased heat that eventually leads to spontaneous combustion.

   O Coal Enhancer inhibits the growth of these bacteria.

   O This is done by adding oxygen molecules to the coals molecular structure, where such bacteria perish when it feeds on oxygen.

Coal Enhancer Enzyme Technology

O Overview

O Coal Enhancer is a biotech enzyme that has been specially engineered for use on fossil fuels. In medical environments and on agriculture.

O The enzyme acts as a catalyst that modifies the substance that it has been applied on, allowing various beneficial qualities to be achievable such as improved production efficiency, reduced greenhouse gas emissions and byproducts.

Bhupindar Singh

Physical Properties of Coal Enhancer

O Coal Enhancer is a specialized enzyme . It is completely organic and therefore a safe-to-use environmentally friendly product.

O Microscopic image of the enzyme (Gram Staining, magnification: 1000)

O Bacteria : 1 – 4 μm

How does Coal Enhancer remove and reduce future accumulation of coking and slag?

O The presence of extra oxygen formed by Coal Enhancer catalytic process actively penetrated into the coke accumulated in combustion chamber walls and surfaces, enabling the residual combustible carbon in the coke to be burned.

O The use of Coal Enhancer creates a higher pH (pH=8.5) environment in the combustion chamber, causing the accumulated coke to separate and lose its adhesive strength.

O Under high temperature (1,100°C), the coke and carbon deposits are loosened from the surfaces, leaving behind a dry solid film that protects the furnace walls from corrosion.

O Carbon deposits reduce the lifespan and output potential of equipment, affecting not only heat transfer, but also seals, air flow, burner nozzle and emissions.

O Through the process of micro dispersion, Coal Enhancer improves coal combustion and feed conditions , and reduction of carbon deposits in the furnace.

O It forms a protective layer that protects burner nozzles an metal surfaces.

O The advanced bio cleaning formula cleans up the nozzle , combustion chamber and exhaust system.

How to use the Coal Enhancer?

O Use the Coal Enhancer by spraying solution 1 and then
   solution 2 onto the coal 5 -7 minutes prior to it being used.

Bioreaction Mechanism of Enzymatic Coal Enhancer

O Spray directly onto the coal, the serial enzymes activate the catalytic bioconversion under ambient temperature & pressure.

- O 1. Bond cleavage: Results in oxidation combustion performance improvement, elevating coal quality.

- O 2. Rapid disintegration: Enable micro-particles to burn more completely.

- O 3. Oxygenate-enriched molecules: Allow Complete combustion under low excess air.

- O 4. Decomposition of impurities: Degradation of carbon fiber, waxes, glutinous stuff, etc., prevents slagging in the burner, feeders, and piping.

- O 5. Transformation: Toxic nitrogen oxides, sulfur oxides turns into non-toxic complex, and reduction in emissions.

- O 6. Eliminating smoke and smog: Flue Exhaust comply with environmental regulatory requirements.

Perlman's Laws of Applied Microbiology

O The microorganism is always right, your friend , and a sensitive partner.

O There are no stupid microorganisms.

O Microorganisms can and will do anything.

O Microorganisms are smarter, wiser, more energetic than chemist, engineers and others.

O If you take care of your microbial friends , they will take care of your future.

O ------ David Perlman, 1980------

Composition of Enzymatic Coal Enhancer

O Composition:

   O 1. Nano-enzyme "enzyme" Group

   O 2. Trace Coenzyme

   O 3. Gene Derepressor

O Physical Properties:

   O 1. Appearance: Active Enzyme Liquid

   O 2. Specific Weight: Approximately 1.02

   O 3. Viscosity: Under 10CPS

Coal Enzymes

- Bio Desulfurization Enzymes

- N-Alkane Dehydrogenase

- MonoOxygenases

- Dioxygenases

- Bio Dispersant (w/o Micell)

- Organometallic Coenzymes

- Aromatic Ring disclosure Enzymes

- Alkyl Degradation Enzymes

- C-C Bond Cleavage Enzymes

- C-S Bond Cleavage Enzymes ...etc.

Enzyme Action

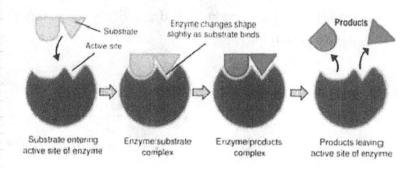

Enzyme Biocatalysis

O Like all catalysts, enzymes work by lowering the activation
   energy (Eat) for a reaction, thus dramatically increasing the
   rate of the reaction.

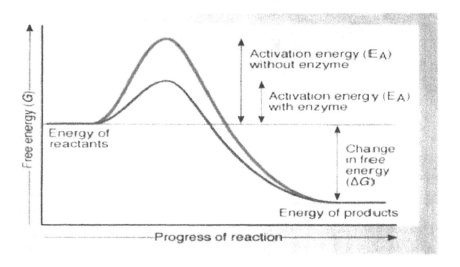

Oxygenases

O Monooxygenases, or mixed function oxidase, transfer one oxygen atom to the substrate, and reduce the other oxygen atom to water.

O Dioxygenases, or oxygen transferases, transfer both atoms of molecular oxygen (O_2) into the substrate.

Chemical nature of the enzymes

O The enzyme's catalytic activity rapidly converts the reactants to a resultants matrix and the enzyme itself is not consumed during the reaction.

O The active site in the enzyme allows such conversion capabilities, the selective active site only functions for a specific reactant, and remaining stable through the transition state.

Bacterial Degradation of Dibenzothiophene (DBT)

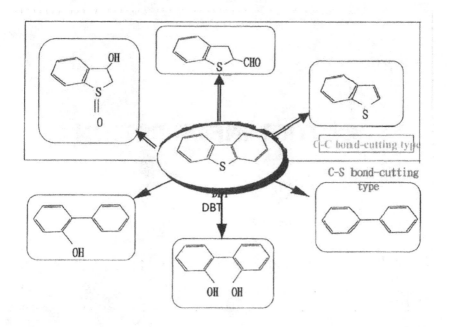

CONTACT INFORMATION

O Aarna Scientific Trust

O Dr. Parshu Ram Niranjan Shastri

   Bhupindar Singh
   1 818 207 1534

CPSIA information can be obtained
at www.ICGtesting.com
Printed in the USA
BVHW031523280621
610633BV00003B/553